FEAR ITSELF
JOURNEY
INTO MYSTERY

WRITER
KIERON GILLEN

PENCILER
DOUG BRAITHWAITE

COLORIST
ULISES ARREOLA
WITH ANDY TROY (ISSUE #626)

LETTERER
VC'S CLAYTON COWLES

COVER ARTIST
STEPHANIE HANS

ASSISTANT EDITORS
CHARLIE BECKERMAN & JOHN DENNING

SENIOR EDITOR
RALPH MACCHIO

COLLECTION EDITOR: CORY LEVINE
ASSISTANT EDITORS: ALEX STARBUCK & NELSON RIBEIRO
EDITORS, SPECIAL PROJECTS: JENNIFER GRÜNWALD & MARK D. BEAZLEY
SENIOR EDITOR, SPECIAL PROJECTS: JEFF YOUNGQUIST
SENIOR VICE PRESIDENT OF SALES: DAVID GABRIEL
SVP OF BRAND PLANNING & COMMUNICATIONS: MICHAEL PASCIULLO
BOOK DESIGN: JEFF POWELL

EDITOR IN CHIEF: AXEL ALONSO
CHIEF CREATIVE OFFICER: JOE QUESADA
PUBLISHER: DAN BUCKLEY
EXECUTIVE PRODUCER: ALAN FINE

PREVIOUSLY

IN THE END, MANY OF THE ANSWERS ENDED UP BEING "LOKI."

WHO HELPED PERSUADE NORMAN OSBORN TO INITIATE THE ATTACK ON ASGARD? LOKI.
WHO CRIPPLED ASGARD'S DEFENSES, LEADING TO ITS ULTIMATE FALL? LOKI.

WHO, WHEN THE TIME CAME, TURNED COAT AND RISKED EVERYTHING TO SAVE THE WORLD
FROM THE UNLEASHED POWER OF THE VOID...ONLY TO BE DESTROYED? LOKI.

AND WHO, THROUGH CONTRACTS WITH HELA AND MEPHISTO, HAD HIMSELF STRICKEN
FROM THE BOOKS OF HEL, SO THAT, EVEN THOUGH HE DIED UPON THE BATTLEFIELD, HE
WAS NOT BOUND TO VALHALLA? THIS, TOO, WAS LOKI.

BUT, DESIROUS OF THE COMPANY OF HIS BROTHER, THOR FOUND A REINCARNATED SPIRIT
OF THE GOD OF MISCHIEF IN THE BODY OF A YOUNG STREET RAT. HE BROUGHT HIM BACK
TO ASGARD, MUCH TO THE CHAGRIN OF HIS BRETHREN, WHO STILL VIEWED LOKI—EVEN A
JUVENILE VERSION—AS A TRAITOR.

NOW, YOUNG LOKI ATTEMPTS TO FIT INTO A WORLD WHERE HE IS LARGELY UNWELCOME...

...AND THAT IS WHERE OUR JOURNEY BEGINS.

JOURNEY INTO MYSTERY #622

The first magpie stopped to mourn. A god's death--even a wicked god like Loki--was no small thing, and a bird's heart--the smallest of things-- couldn't hope to contain it.

The rest? They flew on.

The second magpie left after days at sea. The magpie knew oceans are endless and all oceans are one. So on one shore there would be the beach where, in his youth he saw the hen who left him eternally a-flutter.

The rest? They flew on.

They lost the third in Alfheim, where he stopped to feed from the eyes of a fallen elf girl, torn apart like an over-optimistic dream. He couldn't bear for eyes so pure to stare up at an uncaring sky forever.

The rest? They mocked him. "You're not a carrion eater, you fool," they chirped, "You're not a stupid raven, stupid bird," before flying on.

The fourth died of shock, without warning, falling from the sky with an empty breast. Thor had returned Loki to life, to youth. "What was the Odinson thinking?" the magpie choked out in the language of birds before passing.

"I'm sure he knows what he's doing" said another magpie, not entirely convinced, before flying on.

The fifth was shot with an arrow of purest silver when passing through Hela's Valhalla. The silver in Heaven is so pure that he barely felt a thing.

The remaining magpies were getting worried. Yet what could they do but fly on?

The sixth died in hell.

The last?

The last turned for home. (After certain other trips that do not require further elaboration in our present narrative.)

Why did he do it all? A good question. As much as a bird-brain can really know anything, he knew there was logic here. He knew it would make sense to someone--just that the someone was not he.

The heroes won shortly after our magpies left, as heroes tend to do.

The magpie missed witnessing the triumph, but thought it churlish to be aggrieved when in the last seven-times-seven days he had seen far more than he could have ever dreamed possible.

And now it would be he--not one, two, three, four, five or six--who'd deliver his magpie secret to its intentioned ears.

While his journey was over...

...the journey into mystery was about to begin.

Or it could have, if young master Loki was where he was meant to be.

THE SIEGE OF ASGARD

ah.

Of course, speculation illumina[tes] [mo]re mystery of the event. Loki's final stand against the Void is a question to which we have no answer. Why did Loki do it? No-one knows.

oki's [t] Void is have n do it?

IF YOU WANTED TO LIVE, YOU WOULD HAVE HID YOURSELF BENEATH THE RUG OF THE UNIVERSE BEFORE THE FINAL BLOW WAS STRUCK.

YOU CHOSE TO DIE. THAT MEANS YOU WANTED TO DIE. THAT MEANS YOU *NEEDED* TO DIE. THERE IS ONLY "WHY?".

THERE IS ONLY ONE WHO LOKI WOULD SACRIFICE HIMSELF FOR.

YOU SACRIFICED YOURSELF FOR... YOURSELF?

AYE. I WAS A CREATURE OF SPITE AND WILL. I WAS THE GOD OF CHAOS. BUT IN MY CAPRICIOUSNESS, I WAS TOTALLY PREDICTABLE...

NO GOD OF CHAOS WORTHY OF THE NAME COULD STAND SUCH A THING.

I WROTE MYSELF OUT OF THE BOOK OF DEATH. I SLIPPED PREDESTINATION'S NOOSE. ALL I HAD TO DO WAS ESCAPE MY PERSONALITY'S...

AFTER A GLORIOUS DEATH, I WOULD BE FOUND OR FIND MY WAY BACK. A NEW LOKI: A FRESH PAGE WITH FRESH INK TO WRITE A FREE FUTURE.

YOU WENT INTO OBLIVION WITH NOTHING BUT THE HOPE THAT THERE WAS SOMETHING OUT THERE?

OR THAT SOMEONE WOULD SHOW YOU THE PATH HOME?

And Asgard was put to work. All of the Aesir had a task in preparing for this strange battle, as new and unfamiliar as the city Odin had built.

They knew Ragnarok. What was this?

...hose who thought of human needs above godly ...sign were imprisoned for their betrayal...

NO! ODIN! ALL-FATHER! THIS IS NOT RIGHT--

SILENCE, THOR!

And soon, there was no sound of protest; just the clamor of hammer on anvil. The cacophony of coming war...

THERE. THE TASK IS COMPLETE.

Even the coarse iron of Asgard's enemies was beat into more fitting shapes...

"MANY AGES AGO, WHEN YOU AND HE WERE ON THE CUSP OF MANHOOD, THOR HAD SOMETHING OF AN ARROGANT, PRIDEFUL STREAK. HE SAW THE ELVES' CAVALRY AND SUFFERED PANGS OF ENVY.

"THOR SWORE TO HAVE FINER MOUNTS TO MATCH HIS STRENGTH AND CHARACTER.

"AT WHICH POINT, YOU SUGGESTED..."

WELL, BROTHER. THE MEASURE OF THE STEED IS IN THE EFFORT OF BREAKING HIM. TO BREAK A PONY PROVES NOTHING. TO BREAK A STALLION MAKES A GREAT HORSEMASTER.

BUT FOR THOR... WELL, WHAT IS THE MOST STUBBORN OF BEASTS?

"TOOTHGNASHER AND TOOTHGRINDER WERE THE LORDS OF GOATS. THEY WOULD BEND TO NO MAN, GOD, ELF, TROLL OR ANYTHING ELSE.

"WELL, THEY'D BEND TO FOOD. AND PRETTY MUCH ANYTHING WAS FOOD. THEY WERE GOATS, AFTER ALL.

"ANYWAY: IT WAS A LONG AND SHAMEFUL SUMMER FOR THOR."

"IN THE END, HE MADE HIS WAY TO THE LAND OF THE DWARVES, WHERE THEY FORGED HIM THE BREGD-THRALL--A MAGICAL BRIDLE ABLE TO BREAK THE WILL OF ANY BEAST.

"AND IT WOULD HAVE-- BUT TOOTHGRINDER AND TOOTHGNASHER ARE BROTHERS. NEITHER ONE WOULD BOW TO ANYONE WHEN THE OTHER STOOD FREE.

"THERE WAS ONLY ONE SOLUTION. THOR PUSHED BOTH BEASTS IN THE BRIDLE, AND BROKE THE PAIR OF THEM SIMULTANEOUSLY.

"AND ONLY THEN DID HE RETURN TO ASGARD, PRIDEFUL OF HIS GOATEN STEEDS.

"THOUGH IT TOOK A WHILE FOR OTHERS TO APPRECIATE THEM.

"THIS IS THE PERIOD WHERE THE PAIR OF YOU KIND OF DRIFTED APART.

"YOU KNOW--WHAT WITH YOU BEING AN EVIL, MANIPULATIVE GOOD-FOR-NOTHING AND ALL."

YOU TRIED, BUT YOU MUST UNDERSTAND--THIS BRIDLE BROKE *GOATS*. ENORMOUS, DUNG-DEPOSITING BEASTS OF A MOST WILLFUL NATURE.

A MONSTER OF THE PITS ITSELF DOESN'T EXACTLY MEASURE UP.

NO MORE. NO MORE.

JOURNEY INTO MYSTERY #624

Odin's one-eye watched the armory fill. Tools of old were joined with new weapons, ready to spill most ancient blood...

Odin's plan was terrible... but it was the only plan. He knew this, but he picked at it like exactly what it was--an old wound thought healed, but once again open and putrid. It had to be cauterized, no matter what.

He was almost thankful when he was disturbed by urgent word.

Treachery in Asgard. Escapees-- including disobedient Thor. He knew he should let the whip of his wrath scour them all bloody.

Guided by all-seeing Heimdall, he found the conspirators, ready to spirit away the troublesome Thor to his precious Midgard.

Yet Odin was not without mercy.

The boy was addled with love for the humans. He returned the hammer Mjolnir to him and set the Storm Lord forth to stand against the Serpent's chaos.

Yes, Odin was not without mercy...

JOURNEY INTO MYSTERY #625

DIRE NEWS!

YOU'VE ALREADY BROUGHT "DIRE NEWS," LOKI.

DIRER NEWS!

APPROACHING DIREST, EVEN! OUR MISTRESS MUST KNOW!

MY PET, IKOL, WHEN TRAVELING ON HIS WINGLY-FLAPPING WAY, SAW SOMETHING SHE REALLY SHOULD BE AWARE OF...

YOU'RE A VERY PRETTY GIRL, COULD YOU POSSIBLY HELP ME? I WOULD BE EXCEEDINGLY GRATEFUL.

OH, SUCH DAINTY WORDS. I FEEL SOMETHING MOVE, DEEP WITHIN ME.

YOU HAVE SENT HER HURRYING AWAY, AS YOU WELL KNOW. SHE LEAVES LEAH TO RUN HER HOUSE.

I WILL NOT DISTURB HER ON YOUR WORD ALONE.

VOMIT OR BILE, I'D WAGER.

FNNK.

The Lord of Hell--the only Hell that counted, in his opinion-- would provide the best support he could to Hela's domain, her "lesser" Hel. Seven of his Dísir would police her realm against this promised uprising.

The Serpent has some way to provoke an uprising? Then who better than the Spirit Eaters to cow it?

Hela would retire to her central fastness and await. She would neither move against Hell nor towards the Serpent. And to Loki's need, she would pledge her two strong hands--the right hand of Tyr of Battles and the left of humble Leah.

LET IT NOT BE SAID THAT I AM ANYTHING OTHER THAN AN EXEMPLARY LANDLORD.

AND WHEN THIS IS OVER, THEY WILL ENSURE YOU COMPLETE THE REST OF YOUR PROMISES.

The secret alliance against the Serpent was cemented in the suburbs, mere promises tightened with the bondage of magic. The lords of the underworld returned to their domains.

While their seven sisters policed Hel, first sister Brün, Mad Hlökk, Kára of the Twilight and Göndul the Fool would join the trickster for the length of his campaign. And afterwards?

I WILL RENOUNCE YOU. YOU WILL NO LONGER BE INDEBTED TO ME.

GOOD. THIS IS A GOOD DAY.

ANY DAY IS A GOOD DAY OUTSIDE THE PIT. THAT HELLISH LINGERIE WAS TORTURE.

All of which was arranged out of the hearing of Hela, for reasons that will be obvious to the attentive follower of this narrative (i.e. Hela would skin Loki and wear him as a scarf).

Their servants, soldiers and slaves were left behind. Silence ruled.

But day was not right. He waited for the **night** of the day...

The Serpent belly-crawled to the camp of the slumbering ale-sated giants.

And he made his way to each.

And, one by one, he gave them the sleep eternal.

A score save one of giants' throats he tore out that night.

The one awoke to find himself alone.

GODS DO NOT LIVE IN THE SKY. WE LIVE ON THE EARTH. AND YOU DO SO AT OUR PLEASURE.

And he understood the Serpent, and he rightly feared him.

And all who he told of that night did likewise forevermore.

JOURNEY INTO MYSTERY #626

THERE IS REVOLUTION IN HEL, AS WAS FORETOLD.

WHERE, LEAH? HELA'S SUBJECTS DARE RISE UP?

NOT HERS. ANCIENT DEAD HAVE RISEN FROM THE OLDEST LANDS. WAR-DEAD OF THE SERPENT FROM HIS FORGOTTEN WAR.

THEY ARE THOSE WHO WOULD DEPOSE HELA, NOT THE TRUE DEAD.

THE MISTRESS IS SEIZED.

OF COURSE. THE TWISTED SISTERS SHE BARGAINED FOR ARE IN THE OUTER REALMS. SHE IS ALONE.

WE MUST TO HEL--

NO, TYR. SHE HAS CALLED UPON HER VALKYRIE.* HELA WISHED US HERE. SHE WOULD NOT THANK US FOR DISOBEYING HER.

*For more, turn your gaze to New Mutants the 29th.

VERY WELL. WE WAIT.

CURSE YOU, LOKI. WE LINGER WHILE MY MISTRESS IS IN PERIL...

OR ARE YOU SCARED, TYR?

PERHAPS AS SCARED OF THEM AS YOU WERE OF US?

THOR

It was the end of times.
Asgard had fallen at last.

Writer: **DANA PERKINS**   Designer: **SPRING HOTELING**

With the cycle fashioned by Those Who Sit Above In Shadow broken, the final battle — the ultimate Ragnarok — had occurred, and the denizens of the Golden Realm were no more. Thor, the last Lord of Asgard, had sailed off into sweet oblivion, adrift in such things as dreams are made of.

But even the slumber of the gods must end, especially when events are set in motion by dark forces intent on disturbing the sleep of the just. Such was the case when Latveria's imprisoned ruler, Victor Von Doom, saw opportunity in the form of Thor's mighty hammer Mjolnir as it rent the fabric of the Hell in which Doom was imprisoned. Absorbing some of the essence of Thor and the Asgardians as they fell in battle, Doom flung himself in the hammer's wake as it passed him on its post-Ragnarok flight throughout the myriad dimensions. Although unable to grasp the mystic mallet in his effort to possess it, Doom nonetheless was able to breach his infernal prison and return to Earth.

Meanwhile, Mjolnir had landed far from the fields it knew: in the plains of Oklahoma, to be precise. While covert U.S. forces tried to excavate the weapon, Doom again attempted to gain the power of the Thunder God. After a battle between an army of Doombots and the Fantastic Four, Doom himself arrived. Grasping the handle of the storm hammer, Doom made an unsuccessful bid to raise the weapon aloft. At his contact, however, eldritch energies from Mjolnir shot forth to the heavens and lit up the night for miles around. This supernatural spotlight served as a beacon for a person with the initials D. B. on his suitcase tag.

At this mystery man's touch, both he and the hammer vanished in an explosion of light and thunder.

Thus, even at the end of times, the story would begin anew.

During his spiritual sojourn within the Void, Thor encountered the spirit of the long-absent Dr. Donald Blake. The Thunder God's former alter ego inspired him that he was still needed — and that the Asgardians lived on in the hearts and souls of mortals. Armed once more with Mjolnir, Thor fought his way through a host of demons that sought to keep him from returning to the mortal plane; newly garbed and empowered with the Odinforce, he returned to Earth.

After setting up residence in the town of Broxton, Oklahoma, as Blake, Thor traveled miles into the arid flatland. Once there, he used his incredible power to open up a gateway between the worlds and brought the city of Asgard to settle upon the desert plains.

After sorting out the legalities of such actions, including raising Asgard so it remained hovering above the ground, Thor walked the city's abandoned halls. The echoes of his lonely footfalls inspired him to seek out the other Asgardians. His initial quest brought him to New Orleans, where he encountered his former ally Iron Man. After an impassioned exchange both verbal and physical, a battered Tony Stark suggested Asgard be granted diplomatic immunity.

After Stark departed, Thor found the mortal host of Heimdall, faithful guardian of Bifrost, and brought forth his Asgardian aspect. From that point on, the hosts of Asgard were quickly reinstated to their former glory — beginning with the Warriors Three.

Soon after, Heimdall informed Thor of a gathering darkness in the desert between Nevada and New Mexico. Flying to an abandoned fallout bunker, Thor found dozens of human hosts who had been kidnapped from throughout the world by the Asgardian engine of destruction known as the Destroyer. Among them was a beautiful, raven-tressed young woman who claimed she knew Thor.

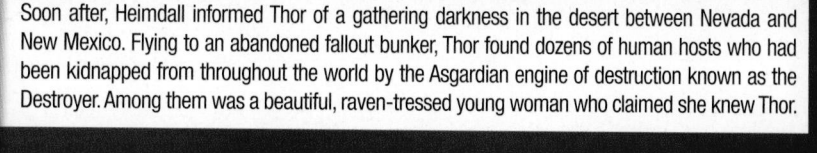

After Thor defeated the Destroyer with a lightning blast that freed the Asgardians, the force behind the Destroyer armor was revealed: Balder the Brave. Balder told Thor it was his anger at failing to prevent Ragnarok that had drawn him into the armor

Along with Balder, there was another surprise awaiting Thor within the confines of that desert bunker. The dark-haired beauty who claimed to know Thor was not Sif as he had expected. It was his foster brother, Loki, returned to life in the body of a woman! After Loki insisted this was a new start for all of them, and that she was trustworthy, Thor reluctantly granted his brother a chance to prove him — or rather — herself.

Loki, alas, showed her true colors almost immediately. While Thor debated with the essence of Donald Blake regarding returning the souls of all the departed Asgardians — including Odin, who Thor feared might desire to stay Asgard's new course — Loki reminisced on a plan he had devised with Doctor Doom. The first layer of an increasingly intricate plot would cause the return of such beings as Frost Giants, Trolls, and evil-natured Asgardians such as Hela and the Enchantress.

With an explosion of sheer power on the cosmic scale, Thor blanketed Earth with divine lightning. All the trapped Asgardians were freed, except for those unwilling or unable to be called back — such as Odin and Sif.

The expenditure of such energy depleted Thor's power, and he was placed within the Odincasket so he could replenish his strength via the Odinsleep.

Once Thor entered this place between life and death, Don Blake materialized and traveled to New York City to see Dr. Jane Foster. Jane had once shared a bond with Sif that was similar to his link with Thor, and Blake hoped Jane could aid him in his search for the missing goddess. There, he encountered one of Dr. Foster's patients: a frail old woman who had been made to host Sif's spirit so Loki could use the goddess' body as his own.

While wandering this Limbo-like realm, Thor found Odin engaged in eternal battle with Surtur. Each day, a wounded Surtur would flee while Odin would die from his wounds, only to be born again the next day. Odin also informed Thor of his awareness of his son's reluctance to call him back from the dead.

Over Thor's protests, Odin told a tale of Asgard from long ago in which a mysterious and powerful sorcerer had turned Thor's grandfather, King Bor, to living snow. Odin had chosen to ignore Bor's pleas for help so he could lead the Asgardians without paternal interference. Odin was then cursed by what he believed to be Bor's spirit, who compelled him to adopt the son of an enemy slain by his own hand: Loki Laufeyson.

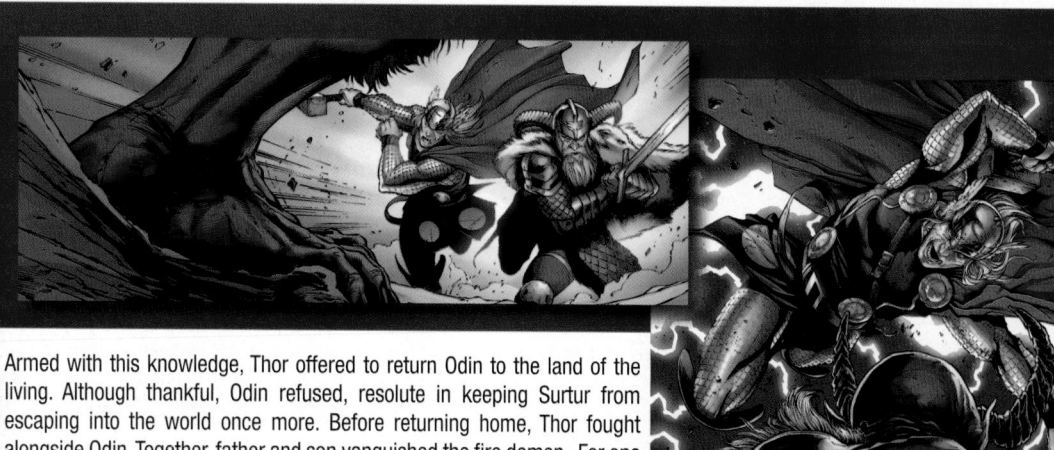

Armed with this knowledge, Thor offered to return Odin to the land of the living. Although thankful, Odin refused, resolute in keeping Surtur from escaping into the world once more. Before returning home, Thor fought alongside Odin. Together, father and son vanquished the fire demon. For one day, at least, Odin did not have to experience death.

Upon waking, Thor emerged from the Odincasket and announced that all the Asgardians who could have been brought back had returned, and that it was time to begin building Asgard's future. This noble goal was put to an immediate test by the shape-shifting Skrulls' invasion of Earth. Aligned with his oath brother, Beta Ray Bill, Thor led the Asgardians to victory in battle against the alien attackers.

Meanwhile, the Mistress of Mischief had been up to her old tricks by sowing seeds of discord among the Asgardians. At Loki's insistence, Balder confronted Thor about the truth of his heritage — and learned he, too, was Odin's son. This news prompted a coronation at which Balder was crowned a prince of Asgard.

The duplicity of the Trickster had never contrasted greater with the Thunder God's nobility than on the evening of the first anniversary of Captain America's death. While Loki stirred the proverbial hornets' nest by telling Balder the Asgardians' adventurous natures were being held in check by Thor's desire to control, Thor summoned forth the spirit of the Sentinel of Liberty in New York City. During their meeting, Thor told Cap that while he had lived many ages and the life spans of many men, the greatest honor he had known had been fighting by Cap's side and calling him his friend.

After honoring Cap with a worldwide minute of silence, Thor returned to Asgard. Due to Loki's meddling, Balder confronted Thor about the unrest in Asgard. The Trickster was just getting started, however, and next paid a visit to her daughter Hela in Las Vegas. Hela helped Loki travel to the distant past, where it was revealed that Loki had played the part of the enchanter who had turned Bor into snow. Also, it was Loki — disguised as Bor's spirit — who had commanded Odin to take the son of a king killed by him in battle to make amends for not returning Bor to the living. After further time travel, Loki then met with his younger self and gave instructions on how to act in front of Odin once his father Laufey was killed.

The pieces of her grand plan now in place, Loki returned to the present and summoned forth Bor from the snow. Bor materialized in modern-day New York, his senses hampered by a spell cast by Loki that caused all to appear and sound distorted and monstrous in his eyes. Alerted by Jane Foster, Thor engaged Bor in a tremendous battle that resulted in Bor's death and the breaking of Mjolnir. Loki timed his arrival with Balder so they came upon the scene too late to stop Thor; as such, Thor was exiled for killing the first lord of Asgard.

Upon Thor's exile, Balder was proclaimed king. At Loki's urging, Balder met with Dr. Doom. The villain invited the Asgardians to take up residence in Latveria, a clime more suited to them. Balder accepted. Among the relocated Asgardians was Bill, an Oklahoman romantically involved with the lovely goddess Kelda.

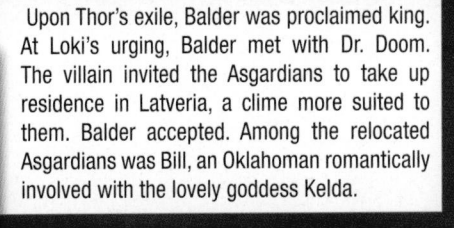

Meanwhile, as Thor began his exile, Jane Foster learned the true state of Sif's spirit and informed Thor. The sorcerer Dr. Strange helped Thor repair Mjolnir using part of the Thunder God's own essence; now, the two are tied together more closely than ever.

Thor made it to the hospital in time to call forth Sif before her aged human host expired. Thor and Sif returned to Oklahoma and joined the Warriors Three, who had exiled themselves to remain with Thor.

Meanwhile, in Latveria, Loki reassumed his old male form, and he and Doom discussed their insidious plans. After Doom sent several Doombots — refitted to hide their true origin — to assassinate Don Blake, Loki provided Doom with a hapless Asgardian warrior so he could begin his experiments on Asgardians via vivisection to discover what provided them with their godly essence.

Bill the Oklahoman learned of their sinister stratagems and attempted to warn King Balder, but not before a group of disloyal Asgardians intercepted him and wounded him unto death. Balder rode up in time to learn of the wicked plan, and he defeated Loki's henchmen. Before he died, Bill saved Balder from one of the Trickster's minions and asked Balder to tell Kelda of his love for her. Learning of Bill's death, Kelda sought vengeance against Latveria's despot. Upon entering Doom's laboratory, Kelda was caught up in the grip of a familiar, massive armored being. As she struggled in vain, Doom explained to her that he would use her divine energies for his own wicked purpose — whereupon her heart was torn out of her body.

The darkness that fell upon the Asgardians in Latveria was nearly echoed in America's heartland with the Doombots' attack on Blake. Only the timely intervention of Sif and the Warriors Three staved them off.

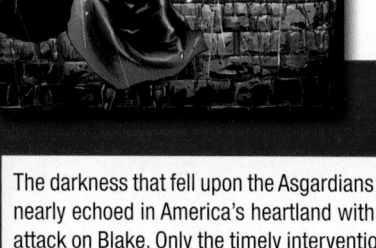

After Heimdall sounded the Gjallerhorn to summon the Asgardians to war, Balder led his forces against Castle Doom. Doom sent his Asgardian abominations, vivisected cyborg monstrosities, against their former comrades and kin. While a horrified Balder and his host battled the monsters, Thor arrived and confronted Doom, who threw Kelda's body down from the stronghold's ramparts. As the appalled warriors looked upon the dead goddess, Loki informed them he could revive her if her heart was returned to her body in time.

As the battle continued, a lightning blast by Thor charged a Destroyer battle suit — the armored figure that had caught Kelda in its unbreakable grip. Kelda's attack on Doom had not fully energized the monstrosity; Thor's lightning granted it full power. Climbing into the armor, Doom attacked Thor. At the same time, Balder retrieved Kelda's heart and destroyed the remaining Asgardian experiments held in stasis. As Thor defeated Doom, who magically disappeared before the Thunder God could land his final blow, Kelda was revived — although still heartbroken due to Bill's death.

Thor and the Asgardians returned to Broxton and Asgard, respectively, only to learn of more disastrous news. For some time, Loki had been influencing Norman Osborn, director of the peacekeeping task force H.A.M.M.E.R., convincing him Asgard was a potential threat that did not belong in the United States. Using Volstagg as a scapegoat, Loki and Osborn sent a group of super villains against the adventuring Asgardian, which caused a deadly explosion that destroyed a sports stadium and killed hundreds of spectators — setting the stage for Osborn's siege of Asgard. Although not at fault, Volstagg was blamed for the destruction; he made his way back to Broxton, where he gave himself up to local police.

This news was only the first herald of disaster, for the Asgardian seer Knut then prophesied Asgard's fall on the morrow. Ever the mischief-maker, Loki dismissed Knut's prophecy and later killed the aged seer. To prevent the ever-vigilant Heimdall from giving warning, Loki magically transferred Heimdall's chambers to the depths of Asgard. After much effort, Heimdall made his way to the surface — but not in time to warn Balder of the impending siege, which had begun with the super-powerful Sentry's destruction of Heimdall's watchtower.

sborn's dogs of war had been loosed — but just when things looked their arkest, the Asgardians found themselves aided by a group of assembled eroes including Nick Fury, Iron Man and the recently returned Captain America.

With the madness of war surrounding them, Loki — without revealing his whole part in the affair — stated Thor was not truly at fault for killing Bor, as sorcery had been at work distorting reality. As victory slipped from his grasp, Osborn commanded the Sentry to lay waste to all Asgard. With a streak of gold, the home of the gods had fallen once more.

Without Osborn to keep him in check, the Sentry reverted to his dark incarnation, the Void. Even Loki was taken aback at the carnage surrounding him, and he sacrificed himself in combat with the Void. With Osborn's forces defeated — among them the clone of Thor, Ragnarok, who was buried when Asgard fell — the Thunder God delivered the final blow and sent the Void to oblivion.

With sorrow at the loss of a once-great hero who had lost his way, Thor gently delivered the Sentry's body into the sun.

In the aftermath of the Siege of Asgard, Balder ended Thor's exile and offered him the kingship once more. Thor refused. With the city's reconstruction under way, the Thor clone was discovered among the ruins. Thor destroyed Ragnarok i battle, thus erasing a lingering taint from the super-hero Civil War. With this dar chapter in the Book of the Nine Worlds finished, a new Heroic Age dawned upo Thor and his people. Along with his closest companions, Thor appeared befor the recently reformed Avengers to give thanks for their help, and proclaime Asgard and Earth to be eternal allies. As a symbol of this newly forged allianc Heimdall's watchtower was placed atop Avengers Tower.

And as a last reassurance, Thor announced that if the call "Avengers Assemble!" rang forth, he would answer.

Yet as the casualties from the Siege were burned on funeral pyres, a warning from Hela cast a somber pall over Asgard. She spoke of a dreadful evil that had returned from ancient times: the Dísir, the cursed Valkyries of Bor, who feast upon the souls of the Asgardian dead.

Since the displacement of Asgard, Asgardian souls had been made to wande such homeless souls were in danger of ultimate annihilation at the hands the Dísir. Due to the machinations of Loki, Mephisto had granted to Hela region in his domain over which she could rule the dead. But the Dísir ha approached the ever-untrustworthy Mephisto and had been granted access Hela's dominion, thus endangering the Asgardian spirits.

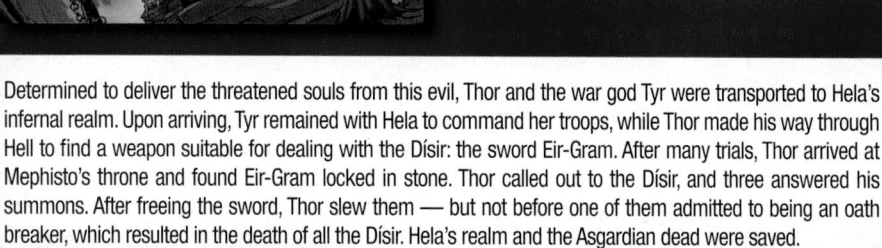

Determined to deliver the threatened souls from this evil, Thor and the war god Tyr were transported to Hela's infernal realm. Upon arriving, Tyr remained with Hela to command her troops, while Thor made his way through Hell to find a weapon suitable for dealing with the Dísir: the sword Eir-Gram. After many trials, Thor arrived at Mephisto's throne and found Eir-Gram locked in stone. Thor called out to the Dísir, and three answered his summons. After freeing the sword, Thor slew them — but not before one of them admitted to being an oath breaker, which resulted in the death of all the Dísir. Hela's realm and the Asgardian dead were saved.

But an even greater threat would soon emerge: the World Eaters. For with the absence of Asgard from its place atop the Nine Worlds, a void has been created that must be filled, and the earthbound Asgard is overrun with those surviving denizens of the remaining Nine Worlds — all of which have fallen to the World Eaters.

Faced with foes more ruthless than any befo encountered, it will take the most drastic actions of — including the return of Loki and Odin — to prepa Thor and his people for the unimaginable challenge th lies before them. But no matter the outcome, one thi is ordained: Thor and the Asgardians will face it w unmatched courage and the promise of future songs glory in their hearts. VERILY!

Art from *Thor* #606 by Billy Tan

HAVE AT THEE, GILLEN!

Kieron Gillen Wielded Mjolnir With Great Vigor.
We Take A Look Back — And Forward — With The Worthy Writer.

BY JESS HARROLD   DESIGN BY SPRING HOTELING

WHEN fan-favorite writer J. Michael Straczynski took his leave from a Thor title he had revitalized, it required a brave man to step into the Thunder God's knee-high, leather-strap boots. Step forward British writer and music and videogame journalist Kieron Gillen. Initially slated as a fill-in writer, Kieron ultimately delivered a popular and critically acclaimed run that lasted for almost a year, setting the scene nicely for his friend Matt Fraction to take over. With Kieron now juggling Uncanny X-Men with Generation Hope, you'd be forgiven for thinking he'd abandoned the Hallowed Halls for Utopia. While you can take the boy out of Asgard, you can't take Asgard out of the boy. The increasingly busy writer is all set to scratch his mythological itch once more — and revive a classic Marvel title, to boot — with Journey Into Mystery. Spotlight dragged Kieron away from his mounting pile of scripts and asked him to bring the thunder. And verily, he doth bring it.

SPOTLIGHT: You took over *Thor* **after one of its most revered runs in years, by one of comics' most popular writers, in the lead-up to the most high-profile Asgard storyline of all time. So, no pressure, right?**

KIERON: After a few days of panicked vomiting and crying, I got over it. Mostly.

SPOTLIGHT: And then how did you feel? Daunted? Inspired? All a-tingle?

KIERON: I presumed my appointment was due to a clerical error deep in the machinery of Marvel that they'd eventually realize. They'd then drag me out, stick me in a pillory and throw sodden back issues at my head. I would be reduced to a papier-mâché statue that would be hoisted up before the entryway to the Marvel offices, as a warning to all and sundry. While I was intimidated, in some perverse way, it almost helped that it was such a big, revered run that had ended so abruptly. In a typical piece of hilariously melodramatic British pessimism, I went into it assuming that no matter what I did, people would hate me just because I wasn't J. Michael Straczynski. And that actually totally frees you. You don't need to worry about whether anyone is going to like it or not. You just worry about the story, and making it as good as you can. And after you get over the flicker of intimidation, you can't help but grin. Thor and his supporting cast are fantastic characters. And I got to sprinkle a little Doctor Doom over the top, just for taste.

Writer Kieron Gillen.

"My fiancée spent the year perpetually bemused, thinking that I was always about to finish this job which never seemed to actually end."
— Writer Kieron Gillen on his year-long "fill-in" run on *Thor.*

SPOTLIGHT: And — the destruction of Asgard on your watch aside — the Thunder God was in safe hands. Your initial fill-in really turned into the little *Thor* **run that could, right?**

KIERON: It just wouldn't stop. It was originally only going to be five issues. Then six. Then they added the tie-in issue *Siege: Loki*, which basically means seven. And then we added a *Siege* aftermath to tie up a few plots for Matt. Then, after the *Thor* office had another look at Pascqual Ferry's deadlines, they figured it would be safer if I did another short arc. Add the *New Mutants* issue I did to tie into *Siege*, which uses Tyr and the Valkyries, and that's thirteen issues. My fiancée spent the year perpetually bemused, thinking that I was always about to finish this job which never seemed to actually end. That's the other thing that made it less nerve-wracking, actually. At any one moment, what I had to concentrate upon was relatively limited. And one of the things I'm most pleased about is that, despite the fact it did expand, the whole thirteen issues absolutely have their own closed themes: the fall and rise of Tyr; Balder facing the duties of kingship; Kelda's grief for Bill; and, of course, the duplicity of Loki cascading toward his death. I don't think it feels like something I was constantly expanding. Also, on a really basic level, I'm happy it sold as well as it did. Capitalism wins!

SPOTLIGHT: You made the transition pretty seamless, building on what had come before, by developing Loki and Doom's relationship, and continuing Kelda's story throughout your run. Was that sense of continuity particularly important to you on this project?

KIERON: It's an ongoing book. I wanted it to absolutely feel like that. I knew what Matt was planning to do. I knew where JMS had left us. With those two landmarks on the terrain, I wanted to plot a route between the two that resolved JMS' directions while preparing the ground for Matt's adventures. Those plots had so much energy left in them that I'd have felt like a bad caretaker of *Thor* without having resolved them. Kelda storming off furiously in the last of JMS' issues is something that needed to be continued. There was so much momentum there, I'd have felt terrible to ignore it. And you try and leave some toys for the writers after you. Reintroducing Tyr was fun, and I'm enjoying seeing Matt play with him, too.

SPOTLIGHT: You really delivered some major character development with those two characters, as well as Loki and Balder, particularly when "Stormin'" Norman Osborn came a-calling. Your book was very much the Asgardian face of *Siege*. The devastation of that story was a great backdrop for you to show the very human qualities of these gods.

KIERON: Absolutely. Since Thor was so involved in the main crossover, I thought it had the opportunity to focus on the supporting cast and how they respond to this tragedy. It's the invasion of Asgard, and *Thor* became the book where you got to see how the Asgardians actually felt about it. The theme beneath it all was basically how all the cast feel they compare to Thor. Thor's the gold standard for Asgardians, in many ways. The arc showed how they all ended up either living up to that paragon or not. That's one reason why I brought Ragnarok in and had him fight Volstagg. On one hand, you've got someone with all the power of Thor and none of the heart. On the other, you've got someone who's nothing but heart. In the end, despite the beating he took, Volstagg is far truer to what really matters than Ragnarok with all his power.

SPOTLIGHT: And you got to crush that dastardly Thor clone, which must have been fun.

KIERON: The job needed doing. *Siege* was the end of the last five years of the larger story of the Marvel Universe, and Ragnarok is one of the biggest symbols of the era. Thor smashing Ragnarok was him bringing the hammer down on everything he represented, as hard as he can. The time for things like him was definitely over.

SPOTLIGHT: Post-*Siege*, you delivered a storyline that not only had two of Marvel's best villains, Mephisto and Hela, plotting and counter-plotting against each other courtesy of the machinations of a third, Loki, but also introduced some devastating new baddies, right out of myth: the god-soul-eating Dísir. They're a great addition to Thor's rogues' gallery, and one we will surely see again.

KIERON: Hopefully. I suspect they're thinking "hopefully," too. Ending up on the ring finger of Mephisto in eternal torment has got to be the sort of thing ladies like the Dísir would want to get out of as soon as possible. They were sort of inspired by necessity. I wanted something to threaten the dead Asgardians in *Siege*, so Dani Moonstar can go and do her Valkyrie thing again. Some kind of anti-Valkyrie seemed logical. So what would they do? Like the time I found myself trapped on

UNDER SIEGE OF LOKI: Thor's wicked stepbrother calmly nurtures the Dísir into existence in the pages of *Siege: Loki*. (Art by Jamie McKelvie.).

a camping holiday with no food, I soon turned to cannibalism. I decided to call them the Dísir — a conflicted, old general Norse term for ancestor spirits — because I hit upon a line saying that there's some research which argues "Dísir" is actually what they used to call Valkyrie before the word was invented. It struck me that instead of making that linguistically true, we could have some fun if we made that *mythlogically* true. As in, before the Valkyrie, there were the Dísir.

Also: Nazgûl Valkyrie. That's an image. So I developed them, including a fair bit of their military organization, for their two appearances in the *Siege* tie-ins, barely any of which was on the page. When I was asked to do another four issues, it struck me as a chance to really let the ladies take center stage. That I'd left them in the ever-supple hands of Mephisto suggested the rest. (I love Mephisto. One of my favorite stories I've done for Marvel is a one-off Doctor Strange tale I did with Frazer Irving that has him being similarly sardonically wicked. He's just a very bad man. At least Loki seems to have an emotional need for what he does. Mephisto's just working his way up and down the list of deadly sins, like a tasting menu.)

SPOTLIGHT: Yum. Judging by both your *Thor* book and your *Ares* series, you know your mythology and your history. What is your background on this stuff, and with *Thor*?

KIERON: My background is basic common-or-garden teenage geek. I read mythology as a child, and what I didn't read I ripped off from role-playing-game manuals. My

In his continuing quest to become Marvel's busiest writer, Kieron Gillen's *Journey Into Mystery* launch will take his tally to three ongoing series. This may be *Thor Spotlight*, but we'd be remiss if we didn't also fill you in on *Uncanny X-Men* and *Generation Hope*. Oh, and a certain one-shot that's bound to "leap" off the shelves.

SPOTLIGHT: How are you enjoying your time with the X-Men? Is Utopia all it's cracked up to be?

KIERON: It's the world's greatest undiscovered holiday resort. Every room has its beachfront view. No Sentinel attacks for at least a week. Perfect.

SPOTLIGHT: And how was working with Matt Fraction? Are you guys more Logan and Kurt or Logan and Scott?

KIERON: It was delightful. Generally speaking, though, we're less Logan, Kurt or Scott and more Dazzler and Pixie.

SPOTLIGHT: Now, you're going solo, and one of the most challenging aspects of writing *Uncanny X-Men* must be making it reader-friendly with such a huge cast.

KIERON: Yeah, that's the thing. When people leave the Avengers, they leave the Avengers. But once an X-Man, always an X-Man. On the other hand, that's a strength. "There are only a few mutants, and they mostly live on this island" is a fairly easy setup to explain. Matt's traditional method has been giving each character an introduction caption whenever they appear. Looking forward, I'm trying to structure stories so that we can absolutely frontload the introductions and have a "roster" for the story in question.
SPOTLIGHT: For all those Gillen completists out there checking out *Uncanny X-Men* for the first time: What one thing do they absolutely need to know, and what can they expect from the book?

KIERON: Their enemies gathered and tried to purge the last mutants

from the face of the Earth. Th[e] X-Men made a stand, and they wo[n]. The question is: What do they d[o] now? They've got what's basical[ly] a small nation, a model communit[y]. They've fought for this. They'v[e] survived. They won a war. Can the[y] now win a peace? They need t[o] learn to *live*.

SPOTLIGHT: Hope and the Fiv[e] Lights. Not a crime-solvin[g] cartoon pop group, but th[e] saviors of mutantkind and star[s] of your *Generation Hope* serie[s]. How is mutant life treating the[m] so far?

KIERON: As you may expect, they'r[e] sort of adjusting to the "hate[d]-and-feared" thing. Hope has th[is] almost religious compulsion t[o] save mutants, and they all fe[el] compelled to follow. They'r[e] basically the flip of X-Forc[e]. X-Force is a black-ops squa[d]; Generation Hope is a search-an[d]-rescue team, midwife to a ne[w] generation. They are also engagin[g] in teenage bonding exercises lik[e] trying to make out with each othe[r].

SPOTLIGHT: And just because w[e] love him, Batroc. *Captain Americ[a] and Batroc #1*. March. Ongoin[g] series a foregone conclusio[n], n'est-ce pas?

KIERON: I'll break the news her[e]: 2012's big crossover is *'Tach[e] Wars*, where Stark, Batroc and a[ll] the other great cultivators of uppe[r] lip fuzz go facial hair-to-facial ha[ir] in the Mighty Marvel Manner. — J

Cover to *Generation Hope #1* by Olivier Coipel.

first Marvel comic I ever read was a *Thor* 1960s reprint, introduction of the Wrecker, which gave me my abiding interest in the man with the head-swaddling and the crowbar.

SPOTLIGHT: The world is about to discover Marvel's Thor. If a non-comics fan asked you what his deal is, what would you tell them?

KIERON: He's about the duality of the mortal and the divine. He's about reintroducing classic myth into the modern world, and gaining all the crazed and furious energy from contrasting them. He's the most important direct line between the modern super hero and the ancient proto-superhumans. They've been telling stories about Thor for 1,200 years now. We're not going to stop.

> "It's driven by Loki, using all his considerable wit and intelligence to keep the Nine Realms safe."
> — Gillen on his new *Journey Into Mystery* title

SPOTLIGHT: Now, as of April, you're the bona fide *Uncanny X-Men* writer. (See sidebar.) It's fair to say your Marvel career is going pretty well at this point.

KIERON: DON'T JINX IT!

SPOTLIGHT: Sorry! But while you have your hands full keeping track of the myriad merry mutants on Utopia, you still have some spare time to spend in Asgard. Word on the street is you're reviving a famous Marvel title of old. What tales to astonish of amazing fantasy will you be suspensefully crafting in the pages of *Journey Into Mystery*?

KIERON: The easiest way to describe *Journey Into Mystery* is that if *Thor* is *Avengers*, then *Journey Into Mystery* is *Secret Avengers*. While *Thor* is acting in bright daylight, *Journey Into Mystery* works by night. It's driven by Loki, using all his considerable wit and intelligence to keep the Nine Realms safe — or, at least, a suitable playground for his own kinds of mischief.

And to do that, he recruits allies, or manipulates foes, to do what needs to be done — ideally, without anyone ever realizing he's doing it. Black ops, Norse-myth style. The first issue starts with one of the biggest mysteries in the modern Marvel Age: "Why did Loki do it?" What was Loki up to with *Siege*? You can see motivation within motivation set up there. If you read it closely, you can see parts of his plan. But...really, what was Loki trying to do by sacrificing himself? If that's been nagging at you, then all is laid out in our first issue. I think people will be surprised. He really thought of everything. Not an entirely stupid man, our Loki. But what's most important isn't what he was thinking, but what he was feeling. And then we go directly into young Loki pulling his team together to do what he has to do in *Fear Itself*. (*For more on Marvel's upcoming epic, see* Fear Itself Spotlight *in March! — Ed.*) Loki's saving the world, and no one will ever know.

SPOTLIGHT: In recent years Loki has been a man, a woman and a teen! Teen Loki — that's enough reason to pick up the book right there.

DOOM UNLEASHED: One of Doom's most vicious and murderous plots in his sordid history unfolded in Gillen's "Latverian Prometheus." (Art from *Thor #604* by Billy Tan.)

SIEGE COMPLETE: Balder, Tyr and Heimdall survey the damage brought by the Sentry's onslaught. (Art from *Thor #610* by Doug Braithwaite.)

KIERON: He works really well as a teen. Loki's always been the god of mischief, which generally speaking has been read in his god-of-evil-aspect. Teen Loki is exploring another way Loki was used mythologically — as in, the boyish trickster. You can have him acting in what's clearly a Loki way, but without the pure force of malice there. In fact, the malice is more aimed *at* him. Understandably, no one trusts Loki. If it wasn't for Thor, you suspect certain Asgardians would have throttled the boy the second he reappeared in Asgard. Immediately, we've got this great underdog dynamic, and tricksters are always best when they're underdogs.

SPOTLIGHT: Who else can we expect to see popping up?

KIERON: Old, dead Loki in issue #1, for a start. Bar him? Anyone and everyone from the mystic realms — and bordering areas — of the Marvel Universe. Long term, that's what *Journey of Mystery* is about: the shadow war between all the mythologies and arcane parts of the Marvel Universe. All the core Asgardians. Some of the Asgardians you won't expect. Norse mythology. Hela and Loki have unfinished business. Tyr. Mephisto. The Dísir. And it's been a while since we've seen Surtur, hasn't it? Looking forward? Dormammu? Strange? Ares? One of the joys of *Journey Into Mystery* is going to be seeing who Loki's going to be dragging in next, while knowing it's a book with a distinct end-point. It's heading somewhere, and when it gets there — well, the book would have to change utterly to continue. It's a big *vision thing*. I kind of got some of the core thoughts of *Journey Into Mystery* from that final arc of *Thor*, "The Fine Print." The idea of doing a book that can mash all these magical and mythological aspects together, and tell of this secret Machiavellian war that influences everything else. The deals that Hela and Mephisto make, beneath the table. And in Loki, we have a character that is a little more flexible ethically than most heroes, so we're able to slip between all these worlds. One part *Tintin*; one part *I, Claudius*; one part *Magnificent Seven*; one part *Sandman*; one part *Queen & Country*, all parts spangly. That's *Journey Into Mystery*. I know it's a clichéd thing for a writer to say, but I think *Journey Into Mystery* is the strongest book I've done for Marvel. There's nothing quite like it out there, I think.

SPOTLIGHT: With you writing both *Uncanny* and *JIM*, is there any chance of some interaction down the line? "Mutants in Asgard" has worked pretty well before.

KIERON: And with Asgard on Earth, it's certainly easier to do. They just need to take a plane ride to get to Broxton. I've certainly got ideas, but nothing in the immediate future.

SPOTLIGHT: And just so we know where your true loyalties lie: Thor vs. Wolverine. Only one can walk away. Who wins, and how?

KIERON: Thor would win — because it's hard to defeat someone who can destroy the planet you're standing on if they put their mind to it — but Wolverine would lose in a very cool way.

Kieron Gillen's work on Thor *can be found in a series of three trade paperbacks. (See sidebar.) Catch up on those — and, before you know it,* Journey Into Mystery *will be on comic-store shelves! !* Journey Into Mystery #622 — *picking up the numbering of Fraction and Ferry's* Thor — *is written by Gillen and drawn by Secret Invasion: Thor artist Doug Braithwaite!*

ThOR
By Kieron Gillen

Fear, Loath

Writers Kieron Gillen, Robert Rodi And Roger Langridge Explicate Marvel's Trickster God

By Mike Conroy
Design by Michael Kronenberg

He's the Trickster God, Thor's adopted brother and deadly rival, one of Asgard's most villainous residents and a major player in *Fear Itself*. He's Loki, a Norse deity who's spread malice and mischief throughout the Marvel Universe ever since Stan Lee and Jack Kirby introduced him in 1962's *Journey into Mystery #85*.

With *Fear Itself* looming, a brain trust of Marvel writers with recent ties to Odin's adopted offspring offered their opinions on what makes this son of a Frost Giant such a terrifying threat and an apt player in an event that's bringing dread to the M.U.

"Loki was always God of Mischief," said Kieron Gillen, who's spotlighting Loki's involvement in *Fear Itself* beginning in the April-shipping *Journey into Mystery #622*. "Fear is one of the prime tools in his toolbox. Even in the most benevolent mischief – a practical joke – it's fear that gives it the spice, and the removal of fear is its punch line. And as anyone who's been reading Marvel comics across the recent decades knows, it's rare that Loki's doing anything toward that end of mischief. But I think the greatest use of fear that Loki has is that his peers don't fear him *enough*.

"They know he's bad," said the British writer, who followed J. Michael Straczynski with a highly acclaimed year-long run on *Thor*. "They know he's done terrible things. But he's always found a way to wriggle free and come off cleaner than any sane mind would expect. He's a magical liar; the world is his web, and everyone was caught in it – and they never realized it. They should fear him more, and that's an incredible reason for why we should be afraid of what he could do.

Cover art to *Journey into Mystery #623* by Stephanie Hans.

"That's our older Loki," said Gillen, who also takes over the reins of *Uncanny X-Men* in April in tandem with artist Carlos Pacheco. "With our reincarnated, younger Loki, there's an element of irony. While his older self died in a moment of glory in a disaster, it was a disaster he precipitated. Now that he's returned, everyone *does* fear Loki, thinking it's a scheme of some kind. If Thor wasn't there, Loki would be dead in the night when some aggrieved Asgardian did the sensible thing. He's more actively feared and vulnerable than he has been at any point in his history, which is one of the things I think that makes Loki such a compelling lead.

"The twist is they're right. As the first issue of *Journey* reveals, it *is* all a scheme. Just one entirely unlike anyone could imagine, and it sets Loki on his path of using fear and mischief against *Fear Itself*."

Robert Rodi's credentials for opining on Thor's sibling rival relate to *Loki*, a four-parter he wrote in 2004; more recently, he has authored *Thor: For Asgard* and *Astonishing Thor*.

"What makes Loki so fearsome a figure is that he embodies the principle of misrule: He exists only to subvert…disrupt…destroy. Civilization is a fragile construct, and there are always cracks in its veneer; Loki represents all the forces that threaten to turn those cracks into chasms.

"He exists to unleash everything we strive to suppress, to tear down what we've built, to stir up what we've settled," the *Identity Disc* writer explained. "And he does all this while laughing; that's possibly the most frightening thing about him. He sows ruin and chaos and death, and he delights in it. For him, mayhem means mirth. He can't ever be reasoned with, or even understood. He can only be avoided.

"Except when he can't," cautioned Rodi, whose Mike Choi-penciled *Astonishing Thor* five-parter concludes in May. "Then, God help us."

Art from *Thor: The Mighty Avenger #3* by Chris Samnee.

Offering a slightly different perspective was Roger Langridge, a New Zealander now based in England. "'My' Loki, from *Thor: The Mighty Avenger*, isn't quite the same character as the regular Marvel Universe Loki. With that caveat in mind, though…

"My first thought is that the title, *Fear Itself*, is a contraction of FDR's famous phrase, – 'We have nothing to fear but fear itself' – which is another way of saying that our greatest enemy is a trick our mind plays upon us. A trick…a trickster…aha! (You see where I'm going with this?) So there's that.

"On a more basic level, there's the simple fact that Loki is a character from mythology, with all the dark baggage that goes along with that," the New Zealander continued. "Have you read any of those Norse myths? Deeply disturbing stuff. Baby-eating, incestuous, evil-goat-devouring weirdness. Loki is part of a terrifying world. Furthermore, he's the wild card in that context. He has the potential to transgress the already-transgressive rules of his world. And there's nothing more frightening than something that is totally unpredictable.

"So, yeah. He's so crazy it just might work," concluded Langridge, who wrote and drew 2008's four-issue *Fin Fang Four*.

However you look it, everybody agrees terror accompanies Loki wherever he goes. And Odin's adopted son definitely won't be out of place in an event known as *Fear Itself*. •

Art from *Loki #2* by Esad Ribic.

Come With Us

Since 1952, Those Three Words Have Enticed Readers Onto The Unimagined Roads Of Marvel. By Robert Greenberger
Design by Michael Kronenberg

As the Golden Age of comics was drawing to a close during the late '40s, the most popular genres appeared to be war, Western, crime and – bringing up the rear – horror. Timely Comics, which was evolving into Atlas Comics, continued its tried and true method of figuring out what was popular with readers and flooding the market with such titles. Atlas already was publishing several mystery series, including *Strange Tales,* with short thrills and twist endings when it launched *Journey into Mystery* in June 1952. Russ Heath's cover to the debut issue was noteworthy for its complete lack of cover copy, a rarity.

Journey into Mystery chugged along for most of the next ten years, with dollops of O. Henry-style stories; ghouls, goblins and monsters; and studies on the human psyche. Edited and largely written by Stan Lee, the book boasted an impressive array of artistic talents – including Gene Colan, Russ Heath, John Romita, Jerry Robinson, Dick Ayers, Joe Maneely, Tony Dipreta, Jack Abel, Paul Reinman, John Forte, Mort Lawrence, Sam Kweskin, Jay Scott Pike, Howard Post, Carl Hubbell, Dick Briefer, Bill Everett, Don Perlin, George Tuska, Myron Fass, Vince Colletta, and Doug Wildey.

Journey into Mystery was a casualty when the line contracted in 1957, but was back a little more than a year later; taking one of the precious eight slots the company was allotted by distributor Independent News.

As Lee ushered in the Marvel Age in the fall of 1961 with *Fantastic Four,* he was encouraged to create other heroes, each of whom needed a berth. Lee chose to make Thor the lead feature in *JIM,* beginning with issue #83. The book's hammer-hurling star grew so popular anthology stories running behind the Thor feature – monster fare mostly written by Stan's brother, Larry Leiber – were jettisoned as of issue #97 in favor of the *Tales of Asgard* feature. It was in these pages readers not only met Thor, but also Odin, Loki, Balder the Brave, the Warriors Three, Sif, Surtur, the Destroyer, Ulik and Hela. Longtime Marvel foes the Absorbing Man, Cobra, Mr. Hyde, the Grey Gargoyle, the Lava Men and Radioactive Man all made their first appearances in *JIM,* further marking it as a noteworthy title. There was but one *Journey into Mystery Annual,* a 1965 offering that introduced readers to Stan and Jack Kirby's concept of Hercules and Mount Olympus. And lo, another hero was born. As of issue #126, though, Lee took the unprecedented step of changing the book's title to *Thor*, which it remained into the mid-1990s.

As the Comics Code Authority revamped its guidelines during the early 1970s, it ushered in a new era of horror. Marvel obliged the pent-up demand with *Chamber of Chills*, *Tower of Shadows* and a revived *Journey into Mystery* in October 1972. Along with original terror tales and reprints, the new series adapted works from Robert E. Howard, Robert Bloch and H.P. Lovecraft. Writers included Roy Thomas, Steve Englehart, Steve Gerber, Ron Goulart, and George Alec Effinger; among the artistic contributors were Gil Kane, Jim Starlin, Tom Palmer, Ralph Reese, Billy Graham and Gene Colan, who was also represented in the first incarnation. After five issues, *JIM* switched to all reprints before ending with #19.

Everything changed in 1996 as Thor was among several heroes to vanish at the end of the Onslaught event. Toward the end of the year, *Journey into Mystery* returned with issue #503 and a feature known as "The Lost Gods." Written by Tom DeFalco and illustrated by Deodato Studios, the story focused on the Asgardian gods minus their memories, now living on Earth. The World Tree Yggdrasil had been lulled into thinking Ragnarok had occurred, and that a new cycle of gods was to begin. For the next year, readers saw Sif, Balder, Ulik the Troll, the Warriors Three and the Enchantress slowly regain their knowledge of the past and forge a future for themselves without Asgard to call home. Red Norvell gathered them to prepare them to do battle with Set, the Egyptian God of the Dead.

With issue #614, *Journey into*

Mystery became an anthology, its focus shifting to other heroes from the Marvel Universe such as Shang-Chi, Master of Kung-Fu; Black Widow; and Hannibal King.

Thor returned in 1998, but received his own title and a new #1 under writer Dan Jurgens and artist John Romita Jr. After 85 issues, that title faded; a new *Thor* series began in 2007. It was at this point the Marvel mathematicians took a look back all the way to *Journey into Mystery*'s 1952 origins. They learned that once you counted up the 521 issues of the original run of *JIM/Thor* and added in the second *Thor* series, you were rapidly approaching a 600th issue. So it was that in 2009, *Thor* reverted to the original series numbering. This new status quo remained in place until issue #621, when the God of Thunder left for a new series titled *The Mighty Thor*.

But what of the long-lived moniker *Journey into Mystery*? With issue #622, Marvel handed the reins to writer Kieron Gillen and artist Doug Braithwaite; their focus will be on the newly resurrected young Loki and his relationship with Thor. And so, 59 years after those three words appeared on newsstands, *Journey into Mystery* still has life in it yet! •

Journey into Mystery Collections

- *Marvel Masterworks: Atlas Era Journey into Mystery Vols. 1-3*, collecting *Journey into Mystery (1952) #1-30*
- *Marvel Masterworks: Thor Vols. 1-4*, collecting *JIM #83-125* and *JIM Annual #1*
- *Thor: The Lost Gods*, collecting *JIM (1996) #503-513*

JOURNEY INTO MYSTERY #622 VARIANT
BY **ARTHUR ADAMS** & **LAURA MARTIN**

JOURNEY INTO MYSTERY #623 2ND PRINTING VARIANT